World in Crisis

by Jim Ollhoff

VISIT US AT

WWW.ABDOPUBLISHING.COM

Published by ABDO Publishing Company, 8000 West 78th Street, Suite 310, Edina, MN 55439. Copyright ©2010 by Abdo Consulting Group, Inc. International copyrights reserved in all countries. No part of this book may be reproduced in any form without written permission from the publisher. ABDO & Daughters™ is a trademark and logo of ABDO Publishing Company.

Printed in the United States of America, North Mankato, Minnesota
102009
012010

 PRINTED ON RECYCLED PAPER

Editor: John Hamilton
Graphic Design: John Hamilton
Cover Photos: Jupiter Images, iStockphoto
Interior Photo: Getty Images, pages 13, 16, 17, 19, 29; iStockphoto, pages 1, 4-7, 10-12, 14, 15, 21-27, 32; Photo Researchers, page 9; John Hamilton, page 28.

Library of Congress Cataloging-in-Publication Data

Ollhoff, Jim, 1959-
   World in crisis / Jim Ollhoff.
      p. cm. -- (Future energy)
   Includes index.
   ISBN 978-1-60453-940-0
   1. Power resources--Juvenile literature. 2. Energy policy--Juvenile literature. I. Title.
   TJ163.2.O45 2010
   333.79--dc22
                    2009029865

Contents

Energy and Fossil Fuels

Facing page: Burning fossil fuels pollutes the atmosphere. *Below:* Electricity touches almost every part of modern life.

The world is in crisis—an energy crisis. And the problem will only get worse before it gets better. Humans have an unending need for electricity. We use it to run our computers, to light the darkness, and to cook our food. Almost everything we do requires electricity.

The problem is that in order to create electricity, people burn fossil fuels, in record amounts. These fuels include oil, natural gas, and especially coal. There are limited amounts of fossil fuels buried in the earth. Eventually, they will run out.

Mining and burning fossil fuels creates environmental damage. Burning coal creates ash that is full of toxic chemicals, such as radium, arsenic, and mercury. People who live near coal mines suffer much more kidney and lung disease, which is caused by coal dust and mining chemicals. Also, most scientists believe that burning coal is changing the earth's climate. But coal is so inexpensive, and so abundant for now, that it's hard to stop using it.

What the world needs today is a plan to replace most fossil fuels with cleaner, more renewable energy. It won't be easy, but getting people to kick the fossil fuel habit will have many rewards.

Global Warming

Most scientists agree that our planet is gradually warming. However, there is debate about the reasons for the warming. Most believe it is caused by greenhouse gases.

When the sun's rays hit the earth, some of the heat bounces off. Some is absorbed in the atmosphere, which contains greenhouse gases. A greenhouse gas is any gas that is good at absorbing and retaining the sun's heat. Carbon dioxide, water vapor, and methane are common greenhouse gases. Some of these gases are natural, and others are put into the air by human industry.

Greenhouse gases are important. Without them, the atmosphere couldn't hold enough heat, and the earth would become like a giant ice cube hurtling through space. However, humans are putting too much greenhouse gas into the atmosphere, trapping too much heat.

Facing page: The earth naturally warms because of the greenhouse effect. The surface of the earth absorbs some solar radiation (yellow arrow), and reflects some. The reflected rays either pass back into space, or are absorbed and reflected back by gasses in the earth's atmosphere. Carbon dioxide is a major greenhouse gas. When too much solar radiation is absorbed, the earth warms up, which alters climates around the world.

One of the most abundant greenhouse gases is carbon dioxide. When people burn fossil fuels—especially coal—to create electricity, large amounts of carbon dioxide are pumped into the atmosphere. Most scientists believe this extra carbon dioxide is changing the climate of the earth, making it warmer.

Scientists talk about the earth heating up one, two, or three degrees centigrade. That doesn't seem like much. However, this is the *average* for the entire earth. A few degrees can make a big difference. During the last ice age thousands of years ago, the average temperature of the earth was only three degrees centigrade less than today.

Below: Pumping massive amounts of carbon dioxide into the air is changing the earth's climate.

Some people, on a cold winter morning, will look at the ice out the window and say, "There is no global warming!" However, this is an example of the difference between weather and climate. Weather is what is going on outside right now. It changes from day to day. Climate is what happens all across the world, over decades. When climate changes, it has huge effects.

Scientists aren't sure how high the earth's temperature could rise. It has already risen almost one degree centigrade in the last few decades. The more it rises, the worse the effects could be. A one-degree rise could be manageable. A six-degree rise could be catastrophic.

Below: Changing the average temperature of a region's climate by just a few degrees can result in drastic consequences.

Possible Warming Effects

Below: Millions of people get their drinking water from rivers and streams fed by mountain glaciers, which have been retreating as the earth's climate changes.

There are many effects of global warming, because climate affects every part of the world. Deserts could expand. Food-producing areas could become infertile. Storms, such as hurricanes and tornadoes, could become more severe. Droughts and heat waves could become longer and hotter. Some areas could actually become colder as weather patterns shift, bringing cold air from the polar regions. Glaciers could melt, leaving hundreds of thousands of people without drinking water. Crops and planting seasons could change, which might leave many without food.

One of the most feared effects of global warming is the melting of the world's ice caps, which could potentially flood coastal countries. Some countries could build levees in important areas. But many countries couldn't afford to do that, and millions of people could become homeless.

Perhaps the biggest problem of global warming is that when glaciers start to melt and ocean temperatures rise, the process is hard to stop. Carbon put into the atmosphere today will continue to retain heat for many years.

None of these effects would happen suddenly. While it's possible to see some effects already, others might take 100 years or more to emerge. Scientists agree that the earth is warming. The amount that the temperature will rise, the exact effects, and the degree to which fossil fuel burning is responsible, are still matters of scientific debate.

Above: If rising sea levels flood low-lying coastal areas, many people will have to relocate.

Environmental Damage

Nearly half of the electricity in the United States is generated from coal. While coal is inexpensive, it is the most environmentally damaging of the fossil fuels.

About 40 percent of coal is mined underground. For miners, this is a very dangerous occupation. Injuries and chronic health problems are common.

About 60 percent of coal in the United States is taken from the earth in large open pits called strip mines. Entire mountaintops may be removed, leaving considerable environmental damage.

Right: One of the largest open pit coal mines in the world is located near the town of Korkino, in southern Russia.

Facing page: Modern open-pit mining equipment can extract tons of coal from the earth in a single scoop.

Above: A worker shovels toxic coal sludge from a stream.

When coal is burned at electric plants, ash and sludge are left over. Most of this sludge is piled in landfills and pits without linings. There are toxic chemicals in the sludge, including arsenic, cadmium, mercury, and chromium, which pollute the ground and groundwater.

Air pollution is a problem, too. Burning coal creates toxins in the air. An average coal plant can pump out 10,000 tons (9,072 metric tons) of sulfur dioxide per year. This reacts with water droplets in clouds and creates acid rain. Acid rain can harm trees and vegetation, as well as contribute to people's health problems.

Burning coal also adds other pollutants into the air. These include nitrogen oxide, carbon monoxide, lead, hydrocarbons, mercury, and arsenic.

Natural gas is the cleanest of the fossil fuels, but even natural gas creates environmental problems. Natural gas produces nitrogen oxide, one of the causes of smog and acid rain. Natural gas is also a greenhouse gas itself.

Nuclear power is not usually considered a fossil fuel. Nuclear power produces no carbon emissions or greenhouse gases. However, it produces nuclear waste, a toxic substance that is radioactive. Nuclear waste stays radioactive for thousands of years, so storing it is a problem. The material must be stored in containers that will never leak and never be damaged. Then, that material must be guarded to prevent terrorists from stealing it.

Another problem with nuclear power is the possibility of an accident. In 1986, an accident occurred at the Chernobyl plant in what is today the country of Ukraine. There was a massive radiation leak, and there were many deaths and injuries. The area around the power plant will remain radioactive for hundreds of years.

Below: Abandoned buildings with the damaged Chernobyl nuclear power plant in the background.

A Limited Supply

The world is in an energy crisis because of our dependence on fossil fuels. This is not only because of global warming and environmental pollution. It is also because there are limited amounts of fossil fuels. At some point, fossil fuels will run out.

It is difficult to say exactly how much oil is left. Some oil is easy to extract, but in other places the oil is difficult to access, and therefore very expensive. In some places, the oil is impossible to extract.

Facing page: An oil platform in the Gulf of Mexico. As easily extracted supplies dwindle, companies must drill for oil in places where it is expensive to operate, and where the environment is sometimes fragile.

How much easily extracted oil is left? No one really knows. The oil left in the ground may last 30 to 70 years, but at some point, it will become too expensive to extract. Will some new technology make all oil easy to extract? No one knows.

The supplies of coal are much more abundant. However, continued use of coal means continued environmental damage.

Scientists don't know exactly how long fossil fuels will last. However, almost everyone agrees that the supplies are limited. The world needs to move to more renewable power before fossil fuels run out.

Making the Transition

Scientists estimate that in 20 years, the world's need for electricity will more than double. If everyone knows that a transition to renewable energy is needed, why is progress so slow?

The biggest problem with switching away from fossil fuels is simply that they are a part of so many things we use every day. Cars, trucks, and airplanes all run on fossil fuels. Electric plants mostly run on fossil fuels.

Changing to renewable energy would be very expensive. New kinds of power plants would need to be built. From day to day, it's cheaper to buy a little coal than to build a bunch of new power plants. So, in the long run, it's better to switch. But from day to day, it's cheaper to use fossil fuels. When money is tight, it's difficult to convince people to build new expensive power plants.

But, building new power plants is exactly what communities need to do. They need to make use of renewable sources like wind power, waterpower, and solar energy. New renewable electric plants are needed as the old fossil fuel plants are slowly shut down.

Facing page:
The switch to renewable energy will be costly and take a long time. But as fossil fuel plants age and are retired, wind and solar energy plants will slowly take their place.

Our nation's electrical grid, the system of power plants, transformers, and power lines that move electricity where it's needed, will soon need to be upgraded or replaced entirely. A lot of electricity is lost when it runs through power lines. New low-loss electric lines are needed. A smarter, computer-controlled grid could make use of different levels of electricity. For example, solar power provides electricity during the day, but not at night.

Above: Solar panels on the roof of a private residence.

Net metering is a way for people who generate their own electricity to make money. If a family has a windmill in their backyard, some or all of their electricity needs might be met. If the home doesn't use all of the electricity generated by the windmill, the electric company would buy back the extra electricity. Net metering needs a smarter electric grid and laws that make this possible.

One way to encourage people to switch to renewable energy is for lawmakers to provide tax credits. This means that companies or people who create or use renewable energy don't pay as much in taxes to the government, saving them money. Some lawmakers want to couple this with taxes on carbon and other greenhouse gas emissions. Companies that produce more greenhouse gases would have to pay higher taxes.

Repairing the Damage

The people of the world will eventually reduce the use of fossil fuels and nuclear energy. But will the environmental damage be reversible? Radioactive waste from nuclear power plants may be the longest-term problem. The waste from nuclear reactors will be deadly and radioactive for thousands of years.

Climate change is another long-term problem. Fossil fuel plants are pumping carbon dioxide and other greenhouse gases into the air. Scientists are working on ways to take carbon dioxide out of the atmosphere. In the future, it might be possible to store carbon dioxide underground, or change its chemical makeup so that it no longer is harmful.

Right: Scientists hope someday to take carbon dioxide out of the air and store it safely, or change its chemical makeup into a harmless form.

Climate change is causing many glaciers to shrink. In many places of the world, glaciers are used for drinking water, so their disappearance would be a big problem. Right now, there is no practical way to keep glaciers from melting or to keep the ocean from warming. Perhaps in the future, scientists will find a way.

The earth provides ways to filter many pollutants. Given enough time, the toxins from coal could be neutralized by wetlands and other natural filters. But right now, coal plants are spewing toxins faster than the environment can filter them out. At some time in the future, when power plants no longer use fossil fuels, the natural filters in the environment may be able to catch up and filter out the pollutants.

Below: Given enough time, wetlands can act as a natural filter, cleaning many toxins from our air and water.

What You Can Do

Below: Compact fluorescents use a fraction of the electricity used by incandescent lights.

There is no one cause of this global crisis. Ending it will require many different solutions. There are many things that kids can do to help. Start by paying attention to how much electricity you use. Turn out the lights when you leave a room. Turn off the computer or TV when they are not in use.

Another simple solution is to change old-fashioned incandescent light bulbs to compact fluorescent light bulbs. About 10 percent of the electric power in United States homes goes toward lighting. Fluorescent light bulbs use only a fraction of the electricity of incandescent light bulbs.

Kids can encourage their parents to buy cars that get good gas mileage, which produce fewer pollutants. Hybrid cars and smaller cars tend to get better gas mileage than regular cars and trucks. Plug-in hybrids get very good gas mileage.

Kids can write to their senators and representatives in Washington, D.C., telling them how important renewable energy is to the future of the world. Sometimes, it only takes a few letters or emails for lawmakers to change their minds on important issues.

Also write to city council members. Why can't there be solar or wind power collectors on every building? Do building codes or laws need to be changed? If enough people ask, a city council could make some important steps for the future.

Appliances such as refrigerators, furnaces, and washer-dryers use a lot of energy. Newer appliances use much less energy than older ones. Kids can encourage parents to replace old, worn-out appliances with newer ones that are more efficient.

Above: Recycling is one important way that people can make a difference in saving energy.

Above all, kids can think about what they do. Think about everything. Where do products come from, and how much energy does it take to make them? Can they be re-used or recycled? Can kids use reusable bags at the grocery store instead of getting new paper or plastic ones each time? Does the community recycle? Can the local schools use recycled paper? Can schools get windmills or solar panels? Kids can think about everything they do, and what impact it has on electricity consumption and the environment.

The Future of Energy

The future of energy in North America is still uncertain. Will renewable energy become more common than it is today? Or will electricity generated by burning coal increase, along with continuing environmental damage?

Coal and oil will continue to play a part in the future of energy, at least for the short term. Some people are convinced that coal and oil will always be a part of our energy sources, even if renewable energy becomes widespread.

Part of the solution is to reduce demand. People need to conserve electricity and slow the growth of our appetite for electricity. Research is needed to continue to develop new ways to use renewables and new ways to limit the damage of fossil fuels.

The answer to the world in crisis is to reduce our demand for energy and change our power sources from fossil fuels to renewables. Reduce demand and change sources. However, in a complex world that is built around the burning of fossil fuels, that is a task that is much easier said than done.

The world's future energy needs will probably include a combination of renewable sources, including solar panels (facing page) and wind generators (below).

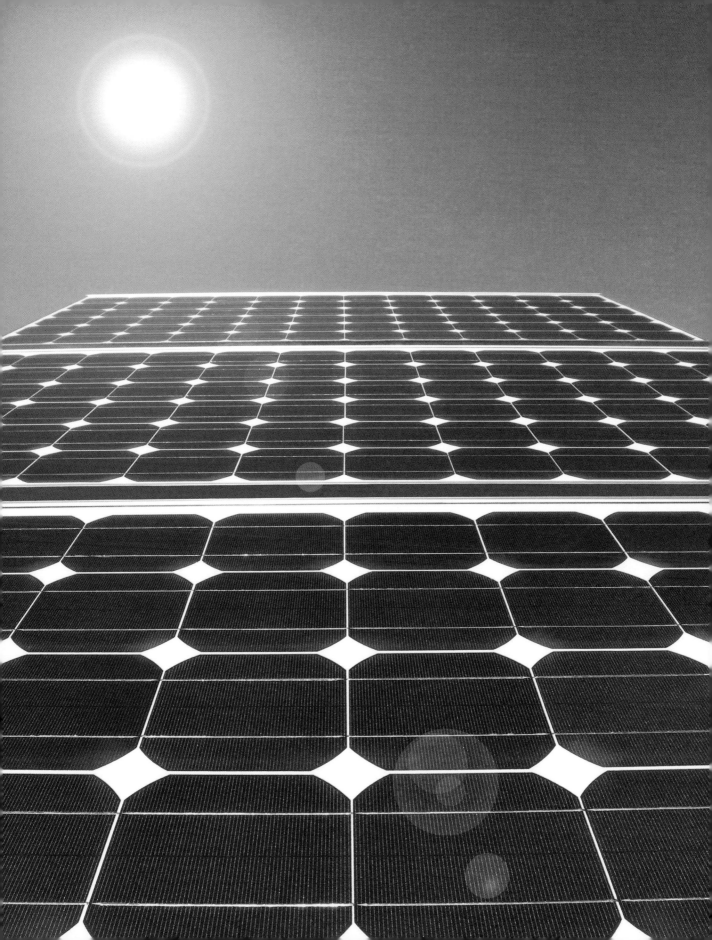

Glossary

ACID RAIN

Rain, or other kind of precipitation, that has a high concentration of acid. It is harmful to plants and many buildings. Most acid rain is caused by burning fossil fuels, which releases sulfur, nitrogen, and carbon into the air. These react with water in the atmosphere to make rain more acidic than is found naturally.

CARBON DIOXIDE

Normally a gas, carbon dioxide is a chemical compound made up of two oxygen atoms and one carbon atom. Its chemical symbol is CO_2. Carbon dioxide in the earth's atmosphere acts as a greenhouse gas.

ELECTRIC GRID

Power lines, transformers, transmission substations, and all of the parts of the system that bring electricity from a power plant into people's homes.

FOSSIL FUEL

Fuels that are formed, over millions of years, by the decomposition of buried biological organisms, mainly dead plants and animals. Oil and coal are the most common fossil fuels burned to create electricity. Burning fossil fuels releases carbon dioxide into the atmosphere, contributing to global warming.

GLACIER

An immense sheet of ice that moves over land, growing and shrinking as the climate changes. Glaciers carve and shape the land beneath them. Glaciers today are found in the polar regions, and in mountainous areas. They hold vast reserves of fresh water. Many cities and regions depend on glaciers for a steady supply of water.

GREENHOUSE EFFECT

The earth naturally warms because of the greenhouse effect. The surface of the earth absorbs some solar radiation, and reflects some. The reflected rays either pass back into space, or are absorbed and reflected back by gasses in the earth's atmosphere. Carbon dioxide is a major greenhouse gas that is produced by burning fossil fuels. When too much solar radiation is absorbed, the earth warms up, which alters climates around the world.

GREENHOUSE GAS

Any gas that is good at absorbing and retaining the sun's heat. Carbon dioxide, which is released into the atmosphere by the burning of fossil fuels, is a greenhouse gas.

NET METERING

The process where electricity is generated by a homeowner, such as by a home windmill. If the windmill generates more electricity than is needed by the homeowner, the electric utility buys the extra power.

RENEWABLE ENERGY

Any kind of energy where the source won't get used up. Wind power, waterpower, and solar power are examples of renewable energy.

STRIP MINING

A way of mining coal that creates a giant open pit, instead of digging underground in mines.

Index